THE PORTAGE POETRY SERIES

SERIES TITLES

Forgive the Animal
Sarah Pape

Love as Invasive Species
Ellen Kombiyil

They Were Horrible Cooks
Allison Whittenberg

The New Life
Wendy Wisner

Restoring Prairie
Margaret Rozga

Table with Burning Candle
Julia Paul

A Bright Wound
Sarah A. Etlinger

The Velvet Book
Rae Gouirand

Listening to Mars
Sally Ashton

Glitter City
Bonnie Jill Emanuel

The Trouble with Being a Childless Only Child
Michelle Meyer

Happy Everything
Caitlin Cowan

Dear Lo
Brady Bove

Sadness of the Apex Predator
Dion O'Reilly

Sparks and Disperses
Cathleen Cohen

Holding My Selves Together: New and Selected Poems
Margaret Rozga

Lost and Found Departments
Heather Dubrow

Marginal Notes
Alfonso Brezmes

The Almost-Children
Cassondra Windwalker

Meditations of a Beast
Kristine Ong Muslim

PRAISE FOR
_____

Users with Access

With the attunement of solemn surrender to all that is, Brandon Krieg overfills the role of poet and presses hotly toward oracle. His felt complicity in the violence of our world qualifies him to access its sublimity: there is no harm or loss here that fails to offer vast and spreading clarity; there is no cruelty that does not contain the possibility of divine gentleness. Krieg doesn't look away. He looks and becomes. These poems permit singular courage, strength, and tenderness—a ferocious fullness for which I am made painfully grateful with each passing, precious word.

—CAROLINE MANRING
author of *Ceruleana*

Brandon Krieg is one of my favorite poets writing today. As I read, I'm compelled to linger with each line, and I'm simultaneously propelled to the next line, and the next, and the next. His imagery--ah! How it understands the heart-shattering beauty of everything around him. I turn to these poems again and again--for their wisdom, and for their ability to see the world with compassion.

—OLIVIA CLARE FRIEDMAN
author of *An Arm Fixed to a Wing*

"It's like this: / ribosome and covenant run on risk," Brandon Krieg alerts us in his tremendous *Users with Access*. Again and again, Krieg's speaker walks us through the corridors and sanctuaries humans have built to hedge against the risk of loving nature. Again and again, he details how these domestic invasions have led us to such folly as the discordant desire to "autocorrect the rain." "Where is life supposed to go?" we're asked. Roofs and clouds alike break across our attention. Half-demolished buildings arch beneath lightning. "Maybe it's / cruel, but here we are," Krieg writes. We're lucky to have Brandon Krieg's poems. His is such a vividly musical attention that we can't help but be taken in by the beauty of it all.

—DAVID WELCH
author of *Book of Echoes*

Users with Access

New and Selected Poems

Brandon Krieg

CORNERSTONE PRESS
UNIVERSITY OF WISCONSIN-STEVENS POINT

Cornerstone Press, Stevens Point, Wisconsin 54481
Copyright © 2025 Brandon Krieg
www.uwsp.edu/cornerstone

Printed in the United States of America by
Point Print and Design Studio, Stevens Point, Wisconsin

Library of Congress Control Number: 2025932496
ISBN: 978-1-960329-86-8

Author photo © Kutztown University
Cover Art: "Landscape XLVI," 2006 © Evan Summer
Etching, Engraving, Drypoint. Used by permission of the artist.

Cornerstone Press titles are produced in courses and internships offered by the
Department of English at the University of Wisconsin–Stevens Point.

DIRECTOR & PUBLISHER   EXECUTIVE EDITORS
Dr. Ross K. Tangedal   Jeff Snowbarger, Freesia McKee

EDITORIAL DIRECTOR   SENIOR EDITOR
Brett Hill   Ellie Atkinson

PRESS STAFF
Sophie McPherson, Ava Willett, Madison Schultz, Paige Biever, Lillian Kulbeck,
Autumn Vine, Mydasia Zipperer

for Colleen and Ezra

ALSO BY BRANDON KRIEG:

Magnifier
In the Gorge
Invasives
Source to Mouth

CONTENTS

NEW POEMS

from INVASIVES (2014)

from IN THE GORGE (2017)

from MAGNIFIER (2019)

NEW POEMS

Afterimagist Manifesto

The snake will not
eat. Too long

a symbol. The god machine's
parts lie
scattered in the field:

antelope horn, mussel shell,
moss beard. In my palm,

this dry rind
of lightning I

recorded from the window of a plane.

Changing Channels

Murder hour blinking
the walls of this room.
If a heron had never come into being
is the shape of my forsakenness.
I have dripped the ribbon
upon itself upon the bed
to make the whorls
of what was larger, have
played with it cutting off
the blood at my wrist.
Above me, roof slates,
gathered long ago from a stream,
are in the rain channeling
impossible sources.

Don't Forgive Me

Morning turns on
its document shredders.
From species to specimen to shreds,
Selah. I've made smudge

of the crawlers and slimers
sustaining. Don't
forgive me, I'll only think less
of you. Just peel the tags

from me where I can't reach,
reschedule ice-ferns on
rut-puddles, redwings
reed-rasping. This is not equinox

after all, it is the much anticipated
Season Six. Please arrange seven
gray gravel piles between me and your aging
hands, the pulse visible

at your inner-elbow, or tears
will blur me. Oh, Godlessness!
You taught us in our rows to demand
more than we got, even

when we were given everything.

Ducdame, Ducdame, Ducdame

I have in common with old window glass
a pleasant warping
of whatever forces through

In this sickly light, the defanged
dogs slurp their sludges. I intone as taught
"Here no mystery is,"

go on dragging the cracked iron bell without tongue,
harnessed to me at birth   rest
clandestinely when I can to listen—

"Authenticity" and "Responsibility"—
the crackle of their packaging impossible to open

Don't please
report my fantasy
of reverse-engineering the old ways
                      last seen escaping
into a canyon just then sunk behind a dam

Brother and sister by dependency,
        our sibling antipathy,
        our little piles

When I tap on my pad
the figures that smother fear   it is you

smiling at me through the glass,
acting out your lives for my enjoyment
just as if I were not there at all,

swiftly reintegrating me

Wrecked Eclogue

Boanerges. Someone asks me on Monday
"How was your weekend?" and I can't remember a thing

I'm lost among the aisles, the displays,
and reach out as if to touch a screen,
as if to "find in page"

I'm writing out a check and I miss the autocorrect
for a word easy as "grace," writing Amazing Graze Church
(I can only laugh, though it isn't even funny to me)

I want it to autocorrect the rain   I want it to autocorrect your face

*

Shantih. I was moved almost to tears by the sale mug's quote:
"If we are gazing at the green leaves of spring,
what have we to renounce?"
and felt ashamed

when you whispered it to me, "what have we to renounce?"
and I saw in your eyes the threshold crossed
when that stubborn gland finally unclenched its cloud
of distance and forgetting, and you were not you, not anything,
a body dropped from the sky onto my body,
a canceled mass canceling me,

and when I could work myself free
I went out to the staircase above the interstate
to let the tidal wash of tires fill my skull,
to find the mountains in their places

on a billboard advertising a Western state

*

Bo. On the call he claimed they could fracture the wellbore
at ten thousand feet for greater extraction,
ejaculating the proppant into the formerly inaccessible
hydrocarbons, boring where no hole was, inducing it
to stay open by
increasing the pressure

and I remembered how the doctor told me he fractured
the tibia and fibula, driving the cobalt, titanium, tantalum
implant home with heavy sledge,

and I thought someday they'll open my coffin
and find that custom joint sitting there
like a grail written over with the runes of my DNA,
and they'll read it and resurrect me whole in a lab, knee and all,
and if they do it right, don't be surprised

if I don't call out your name

*

Sh. After my lunch meeting, a little buzzed, I glimpsed
through stories of smashed factory windows:

the river for loading,
the sky for emitting,

the snow on the pool covers and oaks,
the dripping egg shells and the missing child,

the brass stars on the works, the garlands
on the lintels, nobody starving, everybody recovering,

the teens feeding at the skillets,
the sunset a trick

of stoplights and black cables, the Sundays
recycled of other Sundays,

the news on its loop, so small
I could wear it on my finger, reminder to forget

the sky is to receive
the reactor's cumulus, woodsmoke and meatsmoke,

the river is for loading
vaccines and gaskets, the nationally ranked

surgical ward is for the postmortem all
seem to be reading already and impatient to read

*

Bo. I arrived at the closing early, so
I walked through the wetland sanctuary
sponsored by a competitor company
whose bid had already failed, plot

more or less situated in the shadow of the neighboring complexes,
and couldn't help but remember our weekend trips
when the kids were young, to that lakeside site,

where they waved sparklers around the fire
with Druidic fascination, until Tara waved hers
in the face of the two little ones, and you
stepped in and accidentally burned Maya's neck.

In the morning cold I saw the hundred charred sticks,
paper tanks and bullets, empty bottles of our independence
in shards and shreds on the gravel and blown into the bushes,
and saw a heron in the shallows, the first natural thing,
and thought, *We could have done this all at home*

*

Sh. That's the summer we put the fire pit in our backyard
and made the kids wave their sparklers from different decks
because we couldn't bring ourselves

8

to deny them that simple trick
of potassium perchlorate, titanium, dextrin,

to induce the ungrudging anticipated
dopamine flood—

like when the river from decades of effluents
caught fire,

and a *something else*
lit the faces of the *nothing but*

*

Bo. Where do you want to go
now that the credits have ended

and no credit was given to us?

Sh. Hold my hand again at the canyon-rim beyond
the gas flares on the plain,

name with me the constellations we never learned
as if they had never been named.

Bo. Event Chain, Big Optimizer, Little Already?

Sh. No, Please. Try harder. Pretend you are you and I am me:
Green Gazer, Sparkler Terrace, Burning River.

Bo. But, Shantih, was that us or
was that on a screen?

Sh. I don't know. Sometimes I'm blanked
by what my fingertips think
is left to mean when they tap out their little *l-u-v*s

in the already exhausted
adulthood of the world.

Bo. X-c-h-a-n-ge? X-t-r-a-c-t-i-o-n? X-l-o-v-e? XX
over the eyes after *interval n…*

Sh. No, Please.

Pretend it's me and that I will die.

*

Bo. I pick up a tongueless
shoe on the beach, Shantih.
I will never have been.

Sh. I see tall maples growing
from the roof gutters of the shuttered factory, Boanerges.
I will never have been.

Bo. I could blast the mountaintops and fill the valleys,
Sh. I could slash the forests and silt out the streams,
Bo. I could stack sturgeon on the beaches in piles to burn,

Sh. and Bo. (together) if only to be able to say
I've found what I was looking for: a place I don't care
if I never get back to.

Except—all that has already been done for me.

Staphylococcus and Anaphylaxis

Staph. Your nipples do to me
what robot assassin bees
do geopolitically.

Ana. Even the hairs in your nose, your ears,
appear to be tended expensively.
Even with cheez dust sprinkled on your team gear,
I know posting pictures of you will propagate jealousy.

Staph. The growth mindset lighting your smile reminds me
of mother, touchscreens, and wage slavery,
and is even more leverageable to me.

Ana. Your ambition is like permafrost burning,
blackening glaciers to melt them more rapidly,
spiking my net worth by sinking
the dangerous neighborhoods in the sea.

Staph. Now that you've diversified my portfolio—
from district-renewing condo high-rises to
unregulated mines in nth world countries—
I could overdose on you, insured mightily.

Ana. The way you extemporize haphazardly,
the way you forecast trends so plausibly,
builds in me like an odorless gas.
It will martyr me.

Staph. Cryogenically freeze me.

Ana. To wake embracing thee.

Staph. To landlord Eternity.

Badlands

1.

Oil pumps brainless bird-hammering
Christmas day. At the hill crest:
three snow-bent sunflowers' burnt-out
lamps. The only color in the landscape:
a small oil portrait of a man
leaned against a grave.

2.

Beyond, blue
necks of pheasants
between barbed stalks. The war is far off
in the familiar story
frozen into its words
like cattails in the ditch marshes
wind worries: the pheasant hunters
are far off in the war, the pheasants rising everywhere
in fields the child grandfather walks.
Each shell he loads
explodes in a nimbus of rationed shot
fine as sand, tears freeze to his face
as he walks empty-handed home.
The gray shot ticks softly as it lands
on stalks and snow.

3.

St. John's on Second Street:
winter brilliance does its apostolic trick
to stained glass, bare white Lutheran
arches generations huddle under.
In the silence after the organ's last
sustain, we stand all at once
to pray for those wracked
by loneliness, imagining the 80-mile walk
commanded by Augustus

started at the shuttered dealership
on the windy prairie's edge.

4.

East of town the Cold War
radar towers dark-candle a tabletop butte.
Rumors about homing B-52s,
about the arsenal a hundred miles north,
its warheads oilmen now
tiptoe their wells right up to.
A white horse beneath
the butte's abandoned outbuildings
stamps in a white cloud
of breath beside a snow-capped cylinder
of hay, a pheasant long-glides to rest
at stubble's end where the steep begins:

the very world
annihilated each moment
in a warhead's dream.

5.

Saw Cottonwood Campground,
where he remembers the last
picnic with his toddler brother
before leukemia pulled apart their tiny hands

in the picture of the two of them somewhere
under the blooming trees,
the Little Missouri's silty eternity
behind them blacksilver.

Picture in a box in a closet
on the unfurnished third floor
in his brain. The climb from place to placeholder
chokes him up. When his voice returns he asks
"Did you see the burning coal veins?"

Western

The hunter with
amplifier

plays coyote
calls along
canyon walls.

Each loping
interloper on
owned land dropped is

50 dollars—

"50 dollars a pop"
you could say
and mean it,

or anything,
it wouldn't matter
to the popped dogs

rigored in
truck beds or

hanging
in DNR
freezers, their ears

that flicked
at faintest footfalls snipped
for samples,

meaning—managers
project—more
deer tags, more

temporary positions
stripping coyote
fur for

"rabbit-foot"
keychains.

Planh for this Cycle

Another crowd fired upon—

nothing can be done, so

a crew removes saplings from the margins

Where is life supposed to go?

A mother horse and her colt

face away from each other

tail flicking tail grazing

Ez calls for me in the night

falls asleep against my body

The creek is so dry

we walk where we haven't ever

Frogs leap from our steps

Some kids I'm assuming

don't have to learn as I did

not to crush them with rocks

Ez tripped and was covered

in burrs we picked off

and flicked on the asphalt

Where is life supposed to go?

Later, listening to Dylan,

Ez asked who the devil is

I said a Christian Hades

whom he knows from a book

The man opened fire

on a crowd listening to music

on students learning history

I know it sounds random

The Raramuri I read

breathe intentionally to help

the dancers they are watching

We cannot offer anything

until there are wounded or dead,

then our offering is heroic

and dissected for a cycle

with the hunger for motives,

for a taste of that part of us

We chased the backyard rabbit

until it bolted under the hedge

Where is life supposed to go?

A turtle shrinks in its shell

before it can hear the number

of rounds the shooter had

Ez says the dead opossum

is interesting (interesting?)—

white fur, long hairless tail

The armadillo, too,

cracked open in a ditch—

we rarely see it up close

just moving through its life,

old man wheeling from church,

young woman carrying a hose,

child walking to school

Circumlocution

Vines circle all day seeking a prop
to hook and climb. Silkworms,

their lead silk snipped by researchers,
endlessly obsessively trace

the round bottom of a jar. Maybe it's
cruel, but here we are,

saying: *Close the loop with Finance*, or
Go back where you're from! not *I fear*

white spots popping up again on the scan, I fear
passing the red door will remind me

of what was done there. Ants on a counter
will trace a line of pheromone until you smudge it,

you sadistic fuck, laughing as they scatter
in confusion. Who above us laughs when

gunfire from a high window pulls apart
a tightly packed crowd like gauze?

So much for the universal weave of ballad and basket,
ballot and arm-in-arm march. By the creek, idly,

you pulled back loose bark from a log,
little chest of knowledge, yours to open,

and immediately wasps flew in to rob
the rich cache of eggs frantic termites

clambered to stash in lower tunnels. It's like this:
ribosome and covenant run on risk, advent

or not of branch or post in the vine's
tortuous radius, spiraling

of lines in ballpoint on a page
termites or ants or humans will trace

and trace as if planning to finally arrive.

In a Public Downhill

curtain fluttering in
> no room

wilds
of decay spun back on the spool,
touch chained

> (a fern reads
>> old code)

transmitter tree
transmitter tree

"All is Loneliness" five times on repeat

misses like stereo-
> lithography
>> the white black-

berry flowers in a public

> downhill
>> to sea

Drift

To the tune of *gathering
edible seaweeds*

Drift in the shape of
wood or,
windy,
      your laugh-flag,

            that taut
that taught

the wet pebble its red pulse,
lost when dry—

speckles
      on a red

rock crab's claws,
          tide-

pool sculpin's
fins,

      sands

like sans

Purplish Seaweed

low tide, walk
       where yesterday teens
cast lines to,
  surfperch walked:

     limp damp purplish seaweed
       baking into scent, flopped
         the way waves went,

no renaissance broke through the roof to find
frescoed on the wall
          of the long-buried
              orgy hall

Stranded

Make yourself comfortable between wrecked
        TV sets.
    The little one—hit it
on the left side, shows waves
    arriving on shore. Hit it
                        on the right, see
this loop of a child interrupted
while trying to explain the lump
of baked clay.
                    See such
                            faces streaming
to underground trains,
acorns
rolling down the roof until their weight
rips the gutter off.
Above ground, at a remote stop, cranes lift
cubes of crushed cars
onto an unsolvable gray
                    Rubik's on a barge.
At another stop that church empty of people priced
out of the neighborhood.
            Monuments on the brink of being
demolished regard us like
                    a child realizes
the shirt pulled on is too small
and looks up.
                        You can't say this
to a younger self lost
        where the bridge does
        that angle between the warehouses
and a door set high up in the bricks leads to
                no platform, nothing:
It's precious
        to imagine stepping out
onto that kind of banded cloud-shore you like to watch

from your perch above the interstate,
but soon-forever
          the sonic boom
the scrambled jets make the day the president visits
will crash over you, and you will come up shivering in the
delighted
clapping the tour boats raise above the bay.

Change of Possession

1.

The trail led to rooftops
instead of sea,

a quail in a small pine by a tagged wall
gurgled plaintively

*How Many Locals
Did You Fuck on Your Vacation?*

2.

Lost, I punted
a pinecone over its parent pine

Plainsong

Incense of pencil
shavings speckles
of rain please rest
hatchery century

Those fed pellets (me)
struggle to return
to the source tank
and what we're forgetting

yesses the marshgrass
all down low tide
The dumped chairlift emerges
from surf and the line

for the paper cup
of agates reaches to
where cats climb the shatters
behind the bottle factory

licking and crying—I'm
crushing these fragments
shells, bits, to avoid
being haunted by

a fictional wholeness

Letter to Lost City

Rainsound on that roof
patterned me like a loved voice.
Now every rain takes me
back to the creek swifting down
from the mansion of the newspaper magnate
over golden alder leaves,
proving we can still have something
there is no science of—
a used volume flipped through
at the block-large bookstore, and more, even,
than the translated lovers' grief
at parting, this recipe for
"Wobbly Friendship Bread"
scribbled in the flyleaf.
I copy it for you, friend,
remembering that day lobbing rocks
from the cliff into the sea, musing
we could be in a lost absurdist play
by Aeschylus or Euripides.
Were there such plays?
Were there such blackberries
lining our paths through shore pines
and the scent of burning sand
from the driftwood in the cook stove?
I keep re-steeping the oolong we boiled
on the stove's iron plate, so long after
it tastes only like the water
of this other city far away.

City by the Bay

A friend brines
        red cuts of
        supermarket coho
        in a silver bowl.

He no longer makes
        the mile hike to see,
        beyond the antique
        army barracks,
        the bay and mountains.

Tonight, too much
        Rainier, he realizes he's already
        compared industrial sunsets,
        Tacoma to Gary.

We go silent under
        waves cresting and dissolving
        on the machine upstairs
        that lets his baby sleep.

Fog on Saddle Mountain

Bald of wildflowers on a jutting crag, constant thrum,
I think, of sea,
but you point down, clear-cut's edge, a man in red
is felling firs,
   the thrum his saw's
   engine-sound, and, blind
to red-in-green ghostly numbers
    on optometrists' cards, I wait
for another fir to fall before I find that tiny blood-mite
that sheared the hillside
down to stumps.
      I point
      beyond, a sliver of sand
and sea beneath
a roof of swift approaching cumulous: the flowing surface
of a mimic sea soon surrounding this

lava promontory
jetted once into Earth-wide waters,
held fast now by roots of wildflowers, the only
of their kind to outlast the last ice age.

Brother, I feared you
     would offer me
your savior,
a cloudy face on these cloudy waters
        only you can see.

Instead we both lean over the rail and peer
    into the rolling vapor
islanding us briefly
     beyond the question

whether what outlasts us
    has anything to do with us.

Unintended Use

American Chestnut,
alive but
extinct,

its split-wide spiky nut-jackets like
childrens' numbered folded
paper fates,

tossed away
when the world got old.
Conspiracists say

coconut husks
on Oak Island prove Francis Bacon
was Shakespeare and a Mason.

I say coconut milk in this coffee thermos proves
we are each one of the billions
of helpless Romuluses suckled by globalization.

Chris points to a newt, notes it is the only
vertebrate species that regenerates muscle and bone.
Oh, and when we unlock its secrets soon!

We arrive at the white-domed
mountaintop observatory I was never
invited to shrink the galaxy through, and I remember

Ez and I climbed up here once
in sudden hail, and laughing hid together under
its wooden staircase

listening to the pinging then hush
of hail-turning-snow, warm in our tiny room
heating water for tea on the portable stove.

After a Dream in Winter

Thin snow falls past the cave opening.
Bat squeals quicken   my son's heart,
small as a walnut shell, exquisitely chambered

as the many black shells
rolled in little heaps at the wood's edge.

This morning he woke crying and said
a man dressed as a wall with seven doors
was coming.   Snow out there

is angling into the creek gorge.
What could I say   What could I say

when he asked could we go together
through the same door?

Stars in the Basement

1.

Goofing on Col's feet, Ez slips,
breaks a tooth jagged.

"Get the metal out of my mouth!"

Later, sneaking up on the backyard rabbit, his smile
a new type of smile, new
as the yellow under-wings of the grasshopper flying.

2.

"There are grasshoppers at my school."

He sleeps on his cot in the row.
His chest rises and falls.
His lungs small as an open mussel shell.
His teachers scroll through their phones.

"I suppose the big problem would be
that we would fall down and worship each other."

3.

"Get your words out of my mouth."

Trapped in the basement, a grasshopper's
steady stridulation through the vents,

sound of stars to me, I've got stars
in the basement with the Christmas tree stand,
the washing machine,

but nothing like in winter when clouds part
above the ice crust: that shock
of star silence.

That's like glimpsing through the open
back door Ezra's concentrating face
carefully brushing from the onion shoots we planted

April snowflakes.

Lehigh Gap

May woods, wade,

*

through ferns latticelike shadows, ferns
    the green of a green eye after its bronze-green
eyelid opens

*

Horned moth flickering in trail-dust like
    in a silent film a child's face waiting
    to board a train

*

Dogwood whitely shouts:
    "Canopy is closing!"

Someone has left

*

    a blue-handled broom
    in the old log shelter
to sweep boot rocks
        brought painfully far

*

The trail to Devil's Pulpit closed,
I've ditched anyway all
        "myself am hell"
    melodramas

*

Grasshopper flies up from
    cold fire cairn
    little anti-Promethean
indifferent to bring his coppery blazing down

*

the steep slope to the straightaway river
    traced by parallel ruler lines
of rooftops, switchyard, quarry terraces,
    a far-off gap in woods
 of alternating corn and soy

*

Slope where blackglinting zinc slag
    was dumped—so toxic
trees couldn't decompose at first—
    slope after 40 years
                aflash

with aspens, bluestem, with

*

mourning cloak butterfly
    flapping loopy aimless
redblack joy

*

I antiphonally
    fling my arms as wide
 as an inch is to a lichen,

*

enter the gate of a piney arcade, slip
    on the trail slick with needles,

laugh hard

*

reaching for, falling with, pine branch breaking
onto me holding close to my face
    intricate bronze cones

*

 little temples,
                no,

*

you can't shrink into
    what's larger I
    think, so
                stop

*

at a toppled slab-rock
    seamed weirdly with a white quartz grid
awaiting the next move
    in an omni-dimensional game

*

    My only play: "Test Plot #34"

*

After rock-
colored frog
hops under
rock,

the shock of
the shock of

dame's rocket

Beyond Congratulations

Silence after a great fan
stops whirring

  Leaf-muck
on the unused swing seats,
   broken spider web billowing
  across the string-less guitar opening

Ez asked what the plus signs were
  on all the graves

  A thousand deadfalls
on the trail, we climbed over
   the golden scales of the mushrooms

just as the crickets' wheel
  clicked to a stop

The plusses, I thought,
   could mean anything

Go live on what's abandoned if you can

What Was Continuous

Floodwater overflows the creek into
the pandemic-empty swimming pool

The creek pool that caught my youth-
ful nakedness

is now
the last layer of snow
machined onto the ski slope and groomed

In the city, its melting
will power the simulated sound
of a camera's shutter snapping

What was continuous as wind has gone
discrete-archival

Where a chunk of lintel-stone broke off
above the doorway, a gray wasp nest
does something other

than defy or deify
        completion

Downstream,
  towers gone dark
    loom up out of the sea

Mice do worse

in a maze gazed on by a fake
owl.
    On a nearby hill, meat
hides in sleeping buffalo
                    like work
hides in sleeping me.

"Striving is natural," say
the rule-makers' children. "Dead battery-heavy,"
you said of your heart. "I didn't
taste my coffee," I said, surprised it was gone.

We drove
to the drive-in graveyard,
the window speaker so dead no dead Emerson came on
                to tell us how to rely.

I spoke angry words and heard
        great chunks of the day's cliff
                        crumbling off,

sat still like
a friend after surgery,
        afraid to try the hand
                whose clicking it was supposed to stop.

No-Gate Road

Walnut bark grown over the braid
of wires cut into it   held a gate once
across this thrown-open road

A dragonfly strays
far from water   crackles as it crosses the wide field

I stray to a dew-jeweled thistle's purple
retreat again
to colorless thought

Should have smashed the bottle smashed the glass table
smashed those years ago my face right out of his face

Return to the light
catching this moment everywhere the webs that hold
woods and field together

To even walk through the morning is to
tear the morning apart   little formula
pat as all the little formulas formulas

Trying forgiveness I go grass
has no opposite then eyes closed go wind

For C

The doctor dilated your eyes
and the dumped bedframe in the alley

shined otherworldly white:
all love-work and dream-weight radiating
out at once

not at once
the next day a pale caterpillar
was softening the toothed edge
of a leaf

and your eyes   my eyes   shined again
with that light

elderhand
elderhand

      scare quotes burned off

from INVASIVES (2014)

I, Inc.

I incorporate gneiss and coal and
        long-threaded moss
        and fruits and grains
and esculent roots, a gravity dam
        550 feet high on this
        the continent's steepest
river machine, with 13 other dams, a system
        of locks and
ladders for commerce, continuance

of species, twin
cooling towers of a data-center
        for the world's most powerful
search engine, installed at the site of a lost
        Babel where first
        peoples converged
in that universal language: trade, night-spearing

of salmon by torchlight
        lost (men's faces aflash
        in archives), expressionist
        petroglyphs eerily
        contemporary, photographed
by professors before
        the big sink, I incorporate

with irrigation ditches, thousands
        of gridded miles
of piping, hoses, scaffolding for sprinklers,
        insecticide banners
        over alfalfa terraces greenshining to the edge
        of the glacier-cut gorge,

and on the ridges:
white windmills, futurist

crosses, revivalist
architecture of potato magnates, societies
     for the preservation of automatic, semi-automatic,
     Gun Hill, Gun River, without judgment—
that sucked candy—I incorporate

the leaden
     groundwater under
firing range and echoing
factory, the capful of phosphates,
     Chicago River run backward
     to the Mississippi, algae clotting
the Gulf's left ventricle, plumes of oil filmed
     by unmanned cameras
     designed to sustain
unearthly pressure, ingenious inhibitors
     of serotonin reuptake
present from sewage in measurable amounts
     in the Great Lakes,
     and calm

as the not-I appears, I incorporate
the not-I,

the talkers
in headsets talking to no one present,
Bach and baseball and
     tobacco stocks ticking, the screen-lit
     lotuseating faces staring,
clicking—disgust me, and I incorporate them
     with the disappearing

bees, defense drones
undetectable except
     by ordnance flowering
     skull, sternum, uterus, I am born
     at many removes

from Thoreau, who paused to notice
      the thickness of surface ice,

and, tormented
by his still form in the hut doorway,
sun on skin, outside time, I incorporate it and it binds
      the mettle in my blood,
      the compound sinking
to my feet—impossibly heavy, I drive them

into mountains topped with blinking
towers, ziggurated by
      logging roads, in motley
      of clear-cuts and
necklaced with triple-stranded cables whose buzzing
sounds like rain, and up there
      walking the ancient

Cascade Volcanic Arc, I incorporate
the green company of grunts
      on leave in sunburned skulls, who go
      silent posing
on a high promontory—premonitions
      of Hindu Kush—they frighten me
      with politeness
on the trail, acne, and large vulnerable ears,
I could clap their shoulders, clasp them, pretend to

spar as with my brothers,
but, helpless to keep them
      for their families' sakes
      from disappearing
into the photograph's digital veil, can only
      incorporate them as I must
      these actors charging the hill
      on a screen in a window
I walk under later, many rooms are lit this way,

the allegory literalized, and I am outside

in another cave
of streetlights flicking on under cameras,
I pass through these and incorporate their recordings of me
        into that Gordian nerve-net
        of me not recorded, firing
        charges down too many
        forks to be
        reliably
        modeled, the loops
        of its feedback with external
stimuli so intricately in-nested, a representation

of them would curve its outer ring
        through the Oort,
        and I must go farther,
        into imagined futures, incorporate
cornstalks 12 feet high with black leaves modified
by photosynthetic silicates for 90% efficiency of capture
        and acorn-sized kernels,
        they are beautiful if not yet
        realized, and I am afraid
of them, utterly, as I was in Chicago homesick

for Trask and Kilchis, Siletz and Nestucca, and found,
at the eastern end of Pratt Street where it abuts the lake,
        frozen corpses of
        Chinook salmon
washed up like grotesques out of my memory—
transplants are everywhere, translations of
translations, no place embodies itself, all

overlap, and so I
incorporate them, unifying
them in one brand,
        Brandon, meaning

from a flaming hill
as claimed by a bookmark given me when young—
       I place it in the book of grass
and the book catches fire and illuminates
       the undersides of clouds,
       an advertisement
       like the orange GE
glowing on a building in Midtown
       seen by the lovers
       naked in infinite
       regress of two walls of hotel-room mirrors,

and, full disclosure: it was I positioned against her
       in the mirrors' smallest frame,
feeling I lived in invisible abstract cornucopia diminishment
       of frame within frame where
only images propagate—invincible-distant
as the acronym haloes guarding Mannahatta's skyline—

corporations are all.

Resist or acquiesce; I incorporate
their paltry specializations into this brand
       whose acronym is every star in the night sky,
       and in the day sky too,
       for though it is invisible, it is nevertheless
       present, totalizing, undemocratic
as every corporation aspires to be,

       and, reader far hence,
face lit by a little held charge, a little water's motion,
       a million-stranded rope of sand,
all of my swindling and evasion is for our certain merger,
       for I am corrupt as every other,
       and you must absorb my assets

as I have absorbed this

        broadcast image
from Stalin's Ukrainian famine—the infant automaton
        in the street still nursing on
        its starved dead mother.

Swallow me and go.
I do not wait for you I am in you already.
There is commerce between us.

Processed

I worked at the cannery before coming to this hatchery,
so you can forgive my fantasy

of breeding cylindrical fish without bones
or tails, or scales, or dorsal or adipose

fins—one roll of pink meat machines
could slice neatly to fit tin cans.

It is when I am injecting
smolts with tags computers at the dams will be detecting—

I start to think rather
than each tag transmitting its seven-digit number

to a program predicting adult harvests three
years later, we could save money

by raising these process-ready salmon in holding tanks
without an ocean longing. I imagine the thanks

the governor will lavish on me as we stand
for our picture by the conveyor, at the plant

where I once worked,
watching the pink skinless disks of meat lock

into the waiting socket of each can
with satisfying precision. Then the governor hands

me one of the salmon my daydream has made
as cameras flash, and I see it has no eyes and become afraid.

November

Childwise vision
of a coho thrashing in thin floodwater blankets
on a black road.

Enraged with milt, it slithers over asphalt.
It will not reach the redd;
it will not pass the code
that maps from source to mouth its fluent god.

Yet I return
to its struggle ditch-ward to spawn alone
on the sharp, damp rocks.

This is where I was born.

Levels

Every pit high in the cliff's terraces lives
on the sea's excesses—
sculpins, anemones, small crabs the color of stone

shift and twitch in shallow cragpools   ,
unaware worlds
upon worlds enfold their stratospheres of foam:

star-freaked domes, bald thrall moons
that sway
disturbances in remote elements:

the tidal jets and sprays, for instance,
refreshing these
oases of gill and claw that also fill the dead

crabs' littered, picked-clean
headpieces
with reflections of such wide

miniscule skies.

Invasives

High tide pressed me
up into
      the yellow, invasive
Scotch broom

whose roots hold fast this
crumbling cliff.

Against root-give, I clung
      ever more urgently to the *still,*
small voice—whose seeds

blew into me from 19th century fields—
watching tankers drag

coal hillsides, tourist districts, shining decks
of cars past
      distant peaks,

and since this tide would not
retreat,
cut a hard path up the cliff,
made my way through vacationers

sauntering the green of a fin de siècle
fort. Where genteel, sympathetic

            murder was taught,
in haphazard rows,
children at art camp lounged with ice creams,

laughing avidly. There must be a real
higher or harder
than this, I said,

and took the trail up to a bluff overlooking
international waters,

        walked the rim of the impregnable
        concrete walls of the abandoned

gun emplacements. This is a place, finally,

nothing can invade,
I thought—admiring

        the Mayan-monumentality
        stripped

of deity—I can build hard
        apprehension here.

Up a narrow ladder, I climbed
        into the watchtower,

shut the iron visor, and
        sat in ammonia-smelling dark

where *deep* and *calm* and *perpetual*
could never take.

Then Japanese fire-balloons
                floated elegantly

past the long-range guns
in this afterimage

of a state-park plaque, touching down
70 years ago
        in Montana forests, igniting
        a recent candidate's promise

of colonies on the moon.

Out at the Root

Shore pine on the sea cliff,
perennial axletree on which
stars wheel—waves of the highest

high tide have half-unearthed
its hold. The intricate rootwork
that like sight of the covenant's ark

none should know, hangs exposed:
rain-washed, rope-thick roots scaffold
the vacancy where cliff was, and ends

of dangling rootlets, thread-thin,
pulse droplets like rosaries broken
continually. The upper canopy un-greens

needle by needle; the low notched
branch-ends interlock to gnash
in wind. Even its sudden hush is a harsh

suspension between constellation's cog
and log undressed by waves, ring by ring.
The immanence of no returning

deity inheres in its last distress.
It is a high unblessed scparateness,
at last. At last, it is relentless.

Case Study

In the new buildings
are the old buildings;

in the old buildings
are the felled forests;

in the felled forests
are the forgotten verses;

in the forgotten verses
are the simple arrows

in glass cases
in the new buildings.

Echolocation

These birds are called swallows, these clouds are called cumulus.
Grass grows straight from the roof of the small fortress.
In a film, the murdered ones water a garden.
The flies in the barracks have never heard of Terezín.

Swallow-flight ramifies through the small fortress.
The planks of the bunks don't recall any trees.
The flies in the barracks have never heard of me.
The lindens in rows once meant *hope for peace*.

The mirrors on the walls don't retain any face.
The human is distinguished by reflection and technology.
The lindens in rows once meant *execution-style*.
Guards swam under them in this empty pool.

The human is distinguished by language and memory.
Six thousand graves in rows under linden trees.
Guards peeled the dead up from sticky pools.
Some have said *dead*, others *exterminated*.

Six thousand shadows in rows under linden trees.
One can easily be confused by beauty.
Some have said *holocaust*, a word that means sacrifice.
A brown swallow on its nest inclines its head.

One can easily be confused by hope.
Some have claimed souls can come back as birds.
The prisoner on her knees inclined her head.
The code on the trains meant *No plan to return*.

Some have claimed souls can come back as beauty.
Sixty men in a room, standing in prayer.
The code on the trains meant, *Someone remember me*.
A child stole bread and escaped in a movie.

Sixty men in a room, standing in piss.
My name means war in the language that authorized this.
A child stole bread and was shot in a movie.
I'm not among the murdered, but I feel I should pretend to be.

My name means war in a language that escapes me.
Last night I drank young Moravian wine.
I'm not among the murdered, why should I pretend to be?
The ashes of the bodies were dumped in this river.

Last night I drank *coal-black milk of morning*.
Severed barbed wire hangs down here like nerves.
The names of the bodies were dumped in this river.
Many years later a man is fishing there.

Severed barbed wire hangs down here like vines.
In a film, the murdered ones water a garden.
Many years later a man is thinking there.
These birds are called *never*, these clouds are called *again*.

The Cloisters

Removed from pilgrimage routes,
reassembled across an ocean,
these arches once enclosed the spirit's orders
until death, and housed the bones.

Their placement now reflects, however mitigated
by curators' antiseptic fingers, a magnate's preference—
the rigors of the cross have been dispensed with,
and windows added facing the summer Hudson.

The Sunday crowd looks out, it shuffles through
to see elsewhere the apse, the tapestries kept dark
preserving priceless gilts of cryptic dukes.
A dissected narwhale's horn offers proof
of the existence of the unicorn.

But linger under the rectilinear skylight
that protects from open air these courtyard walls,
and no fleshed-out relic of the word could seem enough
to take the walls again as limits of a life.

Instead a vision comes, of the vast pleasures left
to those freed from laying prayerful bedrock,
and in it, a Rockefeller sadly having his choice
of another stone head, in the purchasable world.

Sundress

This house crouches
under the others' porches.
Its driftwood-gray Victorian

scrollwork is ridiculous
when glimpsed in the total ambush
of rhododendron.

In the door, a narrow window is
hung for blind with a tie-dyed
dress, yellowish,

its sleeves pinned in alleluia position
to the frame's interior. The fashion
is forty years dead,

yet sunlight has so inhabited
the space hips belly and breasts once
lent dimension,

the dress seems to have been
hung here because
sunlight is

the size its wearer was.

Magus

I pick the dandelion's
pointillist eye, blow it blind.

One astral capsule
fastens a spider's zodiac.

The spider, in
concentric meditation,

despite this
interpolation, is

undivided.
I am guided.

Calling

I could go credulous, could call
diminished sixths from the blanching chips
of a mouse's skull;

could take the rushes cased in ice
slow, slow, until the cases' tonic cracking
was fast below in nets of roots;

could loud, like the jay, rip shreds
of moss, richly dropletted, to incorporate
my vanishing;

could swell with the creek to cull
scribbled commandments from lowest branches—transient, yet
influencing the effluence;

could follow in deep leaf-muck
creek's meandering, and find unlooked-for ferns'
green deafening. I sat then,

incredulous, in colors beyond calling, sat
until I picked from the din the heron's eye
that transforms

low fish-bones into long, silent flight.

Preserve

A tall animal has printed the snow drift
on this pond's ice roof.
Incautious to the risk of falling through,
it has crossed. Emerson

assured a version of me more integral
awaits my determination to meet it
in woods. He uses me
to meet himself in woods in me.
On the shoreline, through shafts in the snow crust:
cleft hoofprints, frail blue.

Deer or devil, this creature
walks ungingerly, drops scat freely, peels long strips
of bark from oldest trees, and the trace
its walking makes—doubling and redoubling,
impossible to follow—makes
its way its way.

I stand in dense saplings the hoof prints have split
to cross the pond. Will I find I wait for me
on that other side, or find Emerson only
an echo

diminished to this preserve?
Such a thin roof of ice upholds such wondering.
It shakes and crazes in the human thunders
of planes in descent to O'Hare.

I stand out under the evaporating banners
of others' journeys—Earth is rapidly less than actual
size.

Trace I read in the snow, you are wise.
I must be otherwise.

After Hopkins

Indivisible I divine
        in leaf's veins, lung's blood,
                floodplain, and feathered cloud,
where the all ails, avail.

We've summoned by reduction
        the valenced none, digressed,
                through manias of distinction,
out of reverence, are undeceived

and undone. Therefore, repair.
        Let mountain and meteorite
                accord in scale, write in alleles
aves in human and bacterium alike.

Let us learn to lean again
        on the awe-obstinate phrase,
                like that poor priest who fused
the disparate trout spots,

                cloud colors, into one praise.

from IN THE GORGE (2017)

On the Missouri after Election Day

Rock ring in the road, red-black coals
abandoned by hunters, smoldering in rain.
Empty stand at forest's edge, tree house
where silent grown men sat imagining
the thickly veined necks crowned
with counted points in their crosshairs crumpling.

The billionaire gloating at the podium
spoke straight from his headache to them.
They must have swaggered
into the city, rifles casually swinging,
working themselves up to maybe
burn down the big library,
with its "Co-workers in the kingdom
of culture," its "We shall overcome."

I walk on alone, climb a bank
by the river uniform as though
a bulldozer pushed it there. Beyond it,
on the packed sand, a stack of washed-up
logs too damp to make a pyre of
to send these snagged sandals, cooler tops, and tires
as distress signal up to the empty sky.

My thoughts rise instead, drift
a thousand miles upstream, where men
who looked like me stood smugly on a hill
of bison skulls, posing, having cleared the way
for my great-grandfather to grab a ranch,
build a house modeled after his fraternity
he could line his Harvard Classics up in and be
righteous and white.

At my feet, a sycamore leaf larger than my face
I could bury my face in and weep,

hoping someone on the far bank
might see me kneeling here and say,
"He is not one of the worst, he just lets the worst
make it easy for him, and is ashamed."

I put on the sycamore mask. In this bizarre play,
owl tufts flicked up, I dance this owl dance.
Not of soundlessly plummeting night
for the small pulse, but of lamely hopping,
car-broken in the cage of some nature museum,
symbol of this very human compassion.

I flap against it a little, then I eat from its open hand.

Lapse in Autumn

Find a bare oak branch to walk with like returning
a lopped limb to the painful place,

follow a jagged dry
side creek, rubble heap
of broken amphorae
                into which
lost gods sorted seeds.

A vault in Norway
stores every kind of Earth-seed now
in three-ply foil packages
for mice teeth after us—

so many forms for
passing milk
into the years' revolving mouths,

for the forest to walk through the forest.

Acorn and Bead

Three goslings in green fluff shivering,
the tree frog's bubbled delicate inhaling, the muskrat
pushing up pond's skin with its dark lamp

remind me of you asleep in your crib.
I regret pedaling through a cloud of gnats
because you cried out

when a falling acorn struck your hand.
You wake, bald and pudgy,
a tiny old man.

I remember the "shut-ins"
with their tubes and hanging faces
the church group brought meals to.

I want to be there to bring meals to old you.
You laugh. I laugh,

sliding like a dew bead on a strand of web
far past my own death.

On the Radio I Heard this Storm

that blurred between sweeps
of wiper blades the rolling rural world
and backlit suddenly this door-less
one-room schoolhouse blocked in with bales of hay
was traveling my direction at my speed.

I turned the knob to raise the human voices
above the drilling droplets as one man
who died at 89 today and was being honored confessed
to an interviewer years ago the difficulty of giving up
French horn to compose orchestral works.
I thought I must be passing countless forks

and intersections obscured
by this semi I closely followed,
each leading to some hard-won
hallowed-to-someone ground,

then my attention came to rest again
on the reaching-me-clearly breaking
voice of a woman testifying

she thought fireworks
were going off in a theater,
reached to find her daughter's
arm limp, was pinned

to her by a bullet in her own spine.
The wipers shrieked

suddenly in no rain, and I saw that storm she and I
were caught in traveling

every direction at every speed.

Dusk Fugue

looking down from an overpass
looking up through the canopy
the contrails the sunset
are not different things

the mine and the prison
in the hairs on our heads

your face in my hands,
I see where a canyon
goes too steep for grass

last colors before stars
under the skins of the apples
(dropped in piles for flies)
last colors before stars
in the flies' shimmering bodies

in our bodies bright salmon
stand beneath sunflowers
from our mouths an oak's breath
talks justice at a benefit

the stripped terraces of a mine
mean your voice in my hand
the barred terraces of a prison
mean olives and wine

coordinated sprinklers
keep the coal mounds wet
a phone vibrates a nerve
agent twitches to death
the boy in his father's arms

some will be shielded
by the wave as it passes
somehow my face
is not even wet
my mouth opened and said

mine and prison
apple and fly
sunflowers coal mounds
his boy and mine
the wave and your face
the deaths and the benefits
are not different things

last colors before
the canyon goes
too steep for grass

Verges

On these sands sorrow
is alien, small, dispersible

in all directions as ants
from a gull's skull.

Joy, too, is introduced,

not indigenous, wracked
wig of stems and roots

exposed, with closed inflorescent
eyes. Unison, unison,

dead cry, silenter than sand.

No—to the grass—I say
no—my one sound—

that flashes ten thousand *nows*.

*

In the great grass river,
wind sines silvers,
I wade in.

On the edge in flickers
you are there and
not there, your shining hair

lifts or is lost
in the seething seaming;
one way the river

is green, you are
on the side of silver.
I can't say you are

with me, you are
more than with.

*

Scale by scale,
sand climbs
the acorn cap.

We won't be buried into vaster
scales, I think, and so
hold the fruit until an empty tone

from deepest generation
reaches me,

drop it in my windy
boot print, go

whistling from every edge of me.

*

Wind's sway finds shape
in dunegrass tips.
Thick stalks,

a scatter-plot of
deer pellets. From any
available source, the stalks

take. The wind
through me reveals the intricate
quicksilvers of the short-lived.

*

Eddy in the great
grass river.

Faces flicker,
overlay: you

in a mask of years,
green   silver.

Wind shivers, the mask
falls, you are
there   gone.

*

Nature—I leave it in vaults
of the Late

Standardized, in lovely
19th century books, so others may
achieve by its dismissal

the righteous un-naïve. I walk
sands beneath branching
craze-shapes
like cracks
in the
glaze
of this
brittle blue skybowl lately
unearthed, enduring

in despite of trash, jetwash,
endless highwayside.

I walk in deepest despite.

*

Old symmetry,
easy beauty, let me be.

I also want to know
the drift of speckled weeds
before that widest symmetry.

*

Sassafras sails one
yellow leaf down
the dune's steeps.

It lands on the surface
of the great

grass river—lamp
of contrast,
shy of
symmetry, shining of

its own particularity—
light by which
to find the way back

to this day among days.

*

Haughty ambient
Alhambras malignant
with buttresses, building up

over the sand-road, unaware
of tremulous reflections
where waves vie, the cumulous palaces
glide ahistorical, as if over
the long corridor before birth.

*

Thank brevity gulls race
their shadows over

sand—goodbye—thank brevity
the sole's imprint is blown out
of each footprint and in one

shallow depression
a dried white moth's papery flickers
remind me—thank

brevity for all other than
you: whose day in me is

sand over
sand without
end, whose hours

have broken their glass.

*

Take affirmation, more
difficult than indifference—take it.

Wind-pressed grass tips scratch
worm-tracks in sand windy sand

erases. Pull a tip and follow
the livid arcs it traces.

*

Cumulous palaces
gate the far waters:
pink gold and unison.

I speak into this silvergreen blade
three distinctions

you you you

and float it out—news
of the great grass river.

As Continents Slid

I woke in
cricket dark. He nursed
between us. I'd dreamt,
hanging from eras
over eras, a reservoir
blinked out, savannahs swept
through stanchions
and dry canals,
a quarry was filled and
forested and drowned
at the fault as
continents slid.

I smelled his hair,
kissed his neck.
Yesterday I gave him
a heavy-headed grass stem
pulled from the side
of the tire-rutted mud.
He tripped, dropped
the sunlit grass in grass,
stood and carefully
picked it up again,
acolyte of one afternoon.

The Removes

Lost you where poppies climbed from fields
between houses, where screens on the back of bus seats
showed the living in the now of an obsolescent ship, where a
mandala
and a barcode shared the last wall before the sun set

between houses,   screens
    flashing already like disconnected signal fires:
                        the last wall before
your askance was overwritten

by flashing   disconnected

*

Terraces of semblance

then: roofs like a ruined organ,
sky a wide sustain.

Terraces of
summer, dials

turned to alpenlight.
          A wide sustain

          dials
even us.

Turned to alpenlight:
that   you

fathoms and pervades as

                              day.
Then
fathoms
          opens

*

I, alone, across
the shadow of a fountain falling back curved,
a moment returning vaster
than itself.

    Shadows of   curved
time, the blue in a sepia eye,
               the impossibility
we   met   before

time— the blue in
an arch's sky-through our sign
we have   before
in secret. In truth, anything—

an arch's sky-through—
is only solitude too diminished to lie
in secret in. Truth, anything
I could call you

is   diminished. To lie
a moment   vaster
I call
    alone *across.*

*

A worn down sandstone cliff on the coast,
the path to it crumbled to nothing—
could it have been you and I
there once if there is no trace of it left?

The path
into the applause I thought I heard far off,
          there is no trace of it.
Waves carve the accidental cubism of the cliffs,

the accident   of
our incidence:
          from every angle
the vanishing point passes through the glance.

*

If it could be as never
before, then you. No,
if it could be as always more
piercingly, then through

                you no
word would intervene.
If it could be as always
but with cloudshadow on the dial and no

word
for it in me, then you, and magnified.
But with   no
lake seen through to an altar wrecked

        in me,   magnified
is only a mountain assuming its reflection in a
lake seen
as the picture of itself.

    Only a mountain
piercing   through
the picture of itself
    could be as you.

*

I say you and no one knows what it means.
In the moraine's shadow, I might trace
the vein in your groin as sun touches a stream.

When your hair. When your cusps.
But it is afterward already.

The you of you eludes
even the particular futility of my joy.

I have pebbled an altar to all
aches, and cattails point.
A thousand perhaps directions.

Walls, a wedged bridge, horses browse,
all contingencies parallel except
the vein in your groin as sun touches a stream.

Aches and cattails point.
I have pebbled an altar to all
the you of you eludes—

bald cairn, poor form. Waves anonymize
even the particular futility of my joy.

When your hair. When your cusps.

A thousand perhaps directions
in the moraine's shadow, I might trace,
absolved to tributary.

But it is afterward already.

*

We looked down
on the river from a high window:
nothing else was there in the canyon
where   the sun was always about to set.

On the river
we could see the jade-colored pebbles
wherever the sun was
as if there were no water at all.

We could see
no reflection,
as if there were no water at all,
though the sound was unmistakable:

no   projection of ourselves,
an alien resonance, yet
                          unmistakable
as that you and I were there—

a   resonance
I had not known I had always known, like
   that you   I
saw then as myself. I knelt then in the grief

I had not known I had always known.
Nothing else was there in the canyon.

Lapse in Spring

Crossed dewgrass hillocks
    of the abandoned gravel mine,
wild onion
    on my breath. Picked up white stones
from where ten thousand years ago
glaciers set them down and fled.
    Hands froze.
    Her breasts
under wool, the fine down
on our toddler's rounded shoulders!
    Drove.
On the outskirts, towering
beeches had pushed up through
the glass roofs of the greenhouses.

In the Gorge

At dusk, drove down from the pass, and, cool through the
vents, this smell:

onion fields,
diesel barges,

where the Bridge of the Gods fell epochs ago, its absence in
the glass

of the industrial
waters reflected:

windshields glaring on an arc between two identical states.

I stopped then:
sundown dimensioning

steep basalt walls, onion trucks, tracks of topped stalks,
crying without feeling.

Notes from the Anthropocene

Dust of trains settles on the vineyard.
My hands aren't even good for your body.
The mountains have been miniaturized.
We can't seem to make ourselves vulnerable.
Has the earth been raised or lowered
to become this echo chamber
of domes broadcast on the river?
Olives beneath the stone wall
appear later, pitted, in bowls.
Nothing is required of us.
I'd like to feel genuinely small.
Seed tufts catch on barbed wire.
Gilt scales seal the eyes of the figure.
Fleets sail into future languages.
Our love is too translatable.
Your hands aren't even good for my body.
The gods must have been laughing
to see us touch spicy mouths to genitals,
the hunger not put out.
Or worse, no one was watching.
Confetti speckles the river
falling from who knows where.
The song wheel keeps on spinning
though the singer has long been dead.
Has the earth been raised or lowered
that projectors stream over its faces?
From a hill of ancient grave mounds
we watch the coal plant's candy-striped smokestack
vent strata of earth into sky.
If we could only reside in the sky.
Whatever we do to the earth
the sky becomes more beautiful.

On Not Reaching the Summit

Up there
pixels freeze
cloud-flow
hawk-float
grass-seethe

into a viewpoint
equidistant from every point
on the terabyte grid.
I lie down

beside the last elm
where the path begins to switchback
up a steep headland of
grass grass

and raisin by raisin
eat a handful of raisins
in glad unsuccess
and countless winds

bending one foxglove bell tower
so the shadow of its blackhalo
of bees intermittently
blackhaloes me,

smug as a minor Byzantine
in my niche filigreed
with catchfly, paintbrush, and fescue.

Kings Mountain

Hottest July in memory. Salmonberries already
sweet along the trail. The steeps
where only helicopters could plant fir seeds
after fiery decades
                    are again in entire shade.

I scratch in a spiral notebook
rolled into PVC pipe at 3,000 feet my name
above me always now.
Remembering this will not help me live in a far plains city,
I think.
          Below,
in a rectangular clear-cut, firs at random left standing
cast shadows at exactly the same angle,
analog clock hands synchronized by
some unseen hand, the same

              converting algae into diesel fuel,
              augmenting athletes
              with myoglobin of whales,
              altering the mixture
              of three rivers behind a dam,
              printing an implant
              to hold open an infant's esophagus,
              transforming brains
              into lossless interfaces…

At the highway again, out of water,
I find the trail to the Wilson
behind a windowless van
flanked on either side by prisoners
pushing through tall grass,
bear-like picking berries
the hazard orange of their vests.

They stand at once above the grass
to stare at me in my otherworld
where whatever watches over me
lets me drink from the river whenever I please.

The Oak-Whale

Oak,
sun-lung,
holds its full
inhale longer
than the long inhale
of the blue whale.

I live along the bottom,
never needing
to breach, permeable

to light across
this blood-oak barrier.

Receiver

A condemned house's catalpa
floats orchid-like
white flowers into the road.

On tires pumped with exhalations
borrowed from mussel, chipmunk, bison, brewery, man
lying under a bench wiping his dog's eye with a napkin,
I receive joy prepared for me

forty years ago in France
by workers soldering fast
this ten-speed's diamond frame, listening
to a forgotten match
on a radio now buried beneath a layer of weeds.

No, no
signal longer reaches there.
Yet some resonance rouses me to stand
on pedals, reach into this sun-filled cloud
of downy seeds blowing from the wood beside the creek,
feel the leafy shade cherished by some future traveler
tick my hand.

Beyond the Useful Life

A crow drinks rain from a paint bucket's overturned lid.

Two teens lie on a rock after swimming,
waiting for their cut-off fatigues to dry.

Steelhead suspend inside the cab of a sunken Ford
where the river bends.

A heap of sun-bleached shells shines beside the oysterhouse.

Under three bales of rusted fencing, a garter snake rests.

The barn's last remaining pane flashes as I bike past.

from MAGNIFIER (2019)

Magnifier

Fallen Osage orange smells
like boards at a construction site
I used to climb through
stealing nails I didn't need
The adults laughed at the scream
of lobsters in the pot
Bump stocks and Bibles
said the wind in the trees
Your rewards will be many:
hedge funds and hegemony
I added that last part
after fancy college
Grades tattooed on my ankle
Even the air is ranked
like a snack or a scripture
Maybe you see me as
a black pearl suddenly valuable
I'm the roach in the knife drawer
wearing a mask of white mold
engorged with atrazine
sipped from a dew-bead
my gaze snowed-out
like a robbed carved god
on display for donors
Soon I'll donate my body
to popular culture
to eat me and absorb
these parts per million—
what's left of afternoons
by the spillway under the interstate
taking hit after hit
of oceanic feeling

Comedy of Mirrors

Cinema on the hill: a few frames of rain
without human story.

Born, and the search already ended.

These rampant blackberries introduced
for profit on three taxonomic axes,

this volcanic ash a year in the news cycle
despite so few bodies.

She incredulous: *The falls are left on at night?*

*

And saw from there cloud-shadows on the reefs
where no clouds were, dark shapes perhaps

decommissioned
tanks sunk

to shelter lingcod, cabezon—a discoverable use
waits to absorb each form;
a man dances

behind a signboard as cars pass; after interval n
the program repeats the landscape features:

And saw from there this huge oxidized sun thread the eye
of the overpasses, aware again

as if of a beeping in the house
whose source cannot be found.

*

Like Lost Childhood still wandering the Management Area—

clearcuts, fireweed, fin-clipped steelhead
rebuffed by spillways,

come to rest in an ovoid pool under the structure
erected at the meridian of the fourth and fifth ice advances,

in the center of the salt marshes,
in the center of the brackish marshes,
in the proscenium

whose columns are a succession of ice cores dissolving,
overawing the dams, the audience
wears the masks:

neither cosmic nor tragic but comfortable with the holes cut
for screen's light to access the eyes.

*

And stood under the sulfur flares
and saw from that height to where the subdivision repeats,

remembering the father and the mother
pouring syrups into pools,

the children gazing into the pools.

*

Hot donuts, fried prawns, cold fishwater
swept into drains, the smells

of human breath and low-tide seaweed,
he found a bench under scaffolded totems in a park
above the highway viaduct, watched
containerships haul lost seasons—

Thai rice   Bolivian lithium—

to the orange waiting cranes.

*

And in that city with mountains on either side
she read *Borrowed Love Poems* to him,
and Rilke's letters,
and he kissed the mole beneath her breast:

a pebble among pebbles picked

from the riverbed of childhood, where the hook-jawed gods
washed from sex up onto the shore rocks dead.

And saw from there the source

of the red light on the walls of her tiny studio:
the radio tower on the hill.

And listened to the uncanny broadcast
picked up by her record player as it played:

Bach descending the spiral staircase into
an Iranian centrifuge.

*

And the music stopped,
and the dancers who swayed against each other
long after it stopped
stopped too.

Rilke had been paraphrased
for the vows, and *Borrowed Love Poems* read
under the florist's wire trellis.

He stared into the camera thinking
I will see this picture of myself many years from now

staring into the camera thinking
I will see this picture of myself many years from now.

On this screen it has happened,
the life that seemed my own like a mirror or a garden;

it is a mirror held up to a mirror, a garden held up to a garden;
it belongs to neither the beholder nor the rain.

In Case of Loss

repeat what you can
commute five miles
dismantle the set
rest your buzzed head
against the arch of the storm
your cause is this green
of light in new leaves
petition the pollen
for thousandfold returns
vineyards and pergolas
enduring enemies
make your heart push
blood through your ears
submerged in a tub
tear the certificate
breathe on the glass
see what belief is
the bloody feathers
consult the dry canyons
whose rivers now reign
on thrones behind dams
the stars are reactors
some conglomerate will tap
you won't be consulted
return to ritual
that park always empty
sit under scaffolding
like sparrows or squirrels
neither in nor out
kneel down with your animal
a heartbeat is strange
in any container
step out of the soundtrack
into pine smell and pismires
raying out from a center

return to the verse
marked by another
read it with feeling
to a wall peeling layers
are you a user with access
then enter the portal
sit and say nothing
to a child on the steps
the boardwalks the ice creams
the brainless full summer
knocked down by waves
shell bits in teeth
the hands extended
must be gripped each in turn
placeholder to placeholder
peel off the sticker
put away the pictures
unplug the devices
throw her lock on the eggshells
in the bag at the curb
petition the snows
coming from nowhere
they may bring news
meet her that January
as Physics allows
meet her that June
the pool where crabs scatter
from cleaning the machinery
of the music she loved
each wave rocks it slightly
answer the waves
coming from shores
of nowhere with questions:
you lovers you prophets
which silence is yours?

The Lover in Winter Plaineth

Machines grind wind's fangs
to flour. Piles heap

on the outskirts. I cannot see
to the edge. I creep

again to my niche. I sleep,
fingers triggered
from touching the keys.

Alders wave the river smell
into the hangar. I kneel again to scrape
gilt from illuminations

for re-use. Piles heap
on the outskirts. The outskirts

creep. An orchard could be
in the light at the end of the open hangar.
I cannot see to the edge.

I copy what the dead sang
about the fangs of the wind
though the wind has been defanged.

The piles. The outskirts.
I creep. I sleep.

Reliance Inventory

Extractor by birth, receiver
by nettle petal north of west huzzah buzz

I crumbled the phallus carved into the sea cliff,
listened as wind

etched in the pale palimpsest its Flyleaf of a Thousand Sleeps.

Gray whale boomed, I ran down
the cliff to follow its northbound booming,
feet drumming the packed sand until I had neither

Domestic Tranquility nor The Blessings of Liberty,
the power to coin money, nor to provide and maintain a navy,

and hid my ribs
on the pale underside of a fern.

There, dreamed that on fins
the milk-torch passed through eons,

woke and spied on the Fathers weeping their Leviathan
had washed up on shore, soggy pulp
picked at by beaks

of others,
tagged and collared

herring gull   American shad   pinus contortus
agate   immigrant

blamed for blunt-sparking dry fir needles
(it was white teens with matches

from pornographic matchbox torturing grasshoppers after masturbating).

Old-growth smoke   climax-particles in   alveoli
I get so low

I have to rest every ten steps under
the ash-blackened glacier—
could it be even in these moments melting audibly faster?

where the broadleaf lupine with its fuzzy pods, little pea-purses
packed with enzyme inhibitors does not long sustain

the fantasy one could graze
placidly upon the summer-abandoned ski run blazed purple by it
if one's little bags of California

dates, walnuts, petered out.
I only had to eat two of the raspberry cannabis gummies
I carried with me

to see the stacked cairns
guiding me across countless snowmelt gorges,
across fields of black volcanic powder to my waiting car

worn down to powder and blown away.

Users with Access

Access roads crush their gravels over
   "a mountain where spirits dwell
   "a spring of ceremonial water

Gate code is 1830
   1876 also works
     1890, 1973

"9 out of 10 better dead" to paraphrase
the big stick face carved into the mountain

Heirs have redrawn the district
to include more cottonwoods and junipers
   "It's their own fault for not voting"

Leaf-buds museum prayer beads eternity
will run out of money in 2019
     without more pumps

Put on your mask of instrument panel light,
crack Dakota Kid seeds to stay awake,
   piss in a Big Gulp, toss it in a ditch

Prometheus's descendant
hides in the Killdeer Mountains,
crushed rig hand turned populist,
    liquor picks his liver daily

gas flares gas flares gas flares
  illuminate the canyonland

"We know the Indians
got a bad deal, we watch Bonanza

in the afternoon. She doesn't need
our permission to marry him"

"You can go anywhere,
even off the marked trails"

Like that, I am the first person

to sign in at the box since November,

walk down into the canyon familiar
from the window of the long drives
from my own through my parents' childhoods

My father young near here
                        carried a long icicle
containing all the world's light
home from his route, a little late,
        his father smashed it rightfully against the house

The icicle is whole, doesn't melt, I am
pierced in a dream and no one can tell
I go on in pangs trying to conceal it

rightfully rightfully to the face
in the mountain streaked
        by petrochemical rains,

its burning immobile lips somehow speaking
in the voice of my father's father, saying

"Nothing ever tasted better
        than snowmelt in the canyon trickling
under the bed
of a washed-out road I was repairing."

Riddled Territory

March tenth, record heat. A too positive
Arctic Oscillation
        trapped cold North. Everywhere early
bees cruise—incredulous,
                        I project.
Pollen collects
on hoods of cars. The radio fears
        a last frost
        will sear
leaves, kill crops, or,
                apples, cherries, won't get the night cool
needed to ripen. Cruel how it seems

there are incalculable ways to inhabit
                        airy contingency,
and almost no place to be

                beyond the designated
                        frequencies.
I come close today
        to a hawk's dark
silhouette in the single tree on the grass's edge—
it falls
        to flight, broadcasting
        its shadow across
        the grass-roof, into the root-dens
of rodents—doubtless

stopping them in adrenaline freeze—
        and glides to watchful rest on a branch beyond
Asylum's edge.

A rumored shadow, I think, is our habitual
        dread: talk
of the Palisades Reactor at Covert downgraded,

of possible meltdown,
              risk-benefit, profit—
       a hawk

on the screen in every pocket, our stress-response
              so subtle-constant it lies
              just below the threshold of sense.

I had hoped (warily) something unscripted
here would release me
                     into its urgency,

but the redwing clicks now
like a lighter struggling to finally ignite,
the cardinal echoes with *drop drop drop drop drop*—like
              beads of gasoline
              falling into this dry holographic
fire of purple floral tangles
       that sends up its chemical lavender scent,
and everywhere is downwind

of human diminishment. At last, I think,
I have proven these walks
                     a failure
to dwell upon Earth.
I can excuse myself

from the territory: Asylum
referring only to referring.
              Absolved from caring,

I take the central hill road back,
pause for the first time at
              two weathered wooden birdhouses
beneath a single hill-tree,
see hovering
in the hole of one a delicate wasp, see fallen

                beneath the other a square
                cake of grass frosted
                with gray feathers,
                a nest

I turn over to find it
                        thick with ants
seething to purposes irretrievably beyond

the riddle of *last*.

Coda: Spring

Took the usual path
the other direction   half-hollowed

oak trunk ringed
                    with white half-moon mushrooms held up
one leaf-budded branch in
mist. Went among the least

changes possible to notice,
          to be in other words

what I am regardless of words.
On a scrim of new-green forest one ridge tree in full
whiteflower. I

whiteflower
        with each shout
from the school group's sinuous line below me

that mimics the meadow creek's insouciant crayon-line path
through high grass.
                    I'd forgotten how
to let hand,
          body, boots, gallop
                    in front of intention,
to leave hindsight like a kite caught
in lines
        others left on the sky, to leave
foresight's leveled forests standing a while and not

for the old Romantic lie
          memory of it will make livable the tedium
of a city's rooms,
but because through this web hung now
                    high in canopy-light

this sun-struck eye-lessness, I
dilates.

Walks Scribbled over Scribbled over Walks

Cold hole in my right pant-leg
through which
          grass's eyelash brushes my calf,

flirty infinite

*

I'm shimmery, holographic,
mental projection on a stone church floor labyrinth

by a bored peasant
in a lost epoch
              John Clodpebble
his knack

not for conjuring face-shapes in clouds (commonplace)
but cloud-shapes in faces (wow)

              I'm Son of Clod,
glimpse in a passing face

        burn scars on the sand where the reenactment was filmed

*

I've without even grinding by crawling across continents
my body down found
             the grail Américain:

dry cob in dust, rusty where chewed,
roughish, weighty, ok lob it into

stalks stalks
          ritual?
          yes, unrepeatable

Its arc etches sky with the shell pattern rumored lost

*

Off-trail uphill
snagged and snagged by thorns until
a deer-thoroughfare opens, then:

> *a burr on the haunch*
> *of a cloud, I float around...*

nary a highwayman!

> *tra-la*

I can even pretend

cyber-warriors aren't hunting me in the wireless air

*

Remember Grasmere Gulch?
O subdivided Youth!

I caught Chinook smolts in the big river,

sneaked them in plastic bag plumped with water
past the treatment hut,

poured them out in the creeklet pool
where it burped from its pipe, waited

for the flickers of life,
but

three years later
got my license and had better things to do

than check if any returned from sea

*

I long to let walking be
about the great not-me, but

here's a refrigerator wrecked in a ravine

          and I remember, 8, anxiously awake
at midnight, I was

discovered at the kitchen table
          drawing plans

for the power plant run
by house-sized magnets of opposite polarity

and urged to go back to sleep

*

My legs by their gear-grinding
whir me open   dada contraption
in love with its uselessness

          (eggbeater-cloudbeater)

*

I, Clodpebble the Nth, admit
I was trying to have an experience

So, the bridge in the city of jazz leads to
a gate-less hinge pitted by rust on a post in a field,

I guess there's nothing left to open

          and, as teens with stones
must naturally smash

old plate-glass windows in an abandoned factory,
I smashed the creek ice into tangent panels
with the stick I carry,

was thrilled the next day by
the layered way the fragments had re-frozen

*

What is not information?

(riddle)

my religion's only sacred text

if I had a religion

I'd text it to you

if I had your number

*

I admit I have a religion
THE DOCTRINE AND, and
                              it changes hourly:

now it is a road curving uphill out of sight,
now a bloody feather

I'm not, however,
going to try to fly off into the "circumambient gases"
or tickle infinity, I'll just hunker
            in mud and mend this schism

between the bird imagery faction
            (who prefer the riddle of the whole sky contained
            in an acorn-sized speckled egg)

and the fish imagery sect
            (who say a hundred fingerlings breaking the surface
at once
            escaping some larger thing
            ought to be stamped in metal somehow

on wind chimes and hung in our yards)

Sure, I say, and
        a farm dog tugging with bared teeth at a deer corpse in a ditch
        could be nice in gold stitching
        and a child breathing between gulps of water from a cup
        could be Hymn no.2 in the Hymn Book

What about Hymn no.1?
It would be confusing to have one
in this religion: the congregants are clouds and me
strip by strip peeling
a stick to arrive again at fingertip idiot joy

Don't peace me when I'm in this state!

Your hair will get bark flakes all in it
and your hair is so nuanced and sculpted right now
you look like the antipope
my religion would hire if we could afford it

Will you be our antipope, pro bono, bro?

All you've got to do is walk around looking
like whatever happens next is not

the very thing

Two Notes

walking stick propped
against porch-rail,
vine-circled to the top

*

pings and pings
fabrication plant
              synonyms
for lying gnat-dance

          Peace Walker smelled
river water wick stiff stems,
          a pony bolt
                    in sharp delight

I've gone far
              digging out a vine
    roots entangling
a single note
              buried chime

bullet-heavy packed with dirt,
holding it,
          listening to wind

Sick Georgic

Having neither flock nor hill, forgive me,
I imitate what I do not understand.

The loose tarps rip against themselves in wind.
A grass-overgrown trough is what's left
of the palace complexes.

A dog licks from a drain by votives
still flickering the next morning.

The old man's face suspends there
as the younger lifts up the match:
like that moment when, driving by them,

the rows of stalks go suddenly parallel.

*

Reclamation by drainage reveals
the necropolis. Earrings shimmer
next to brown skulls emerging from mud,

bringing down the angel Curation.

I wear the mark of gold burrs on rolled cuffs,
escape along the dry watercourses

to that square not yet remembered for tears falling
from the tip of the nose onto the touchscreen.

*

Hail on the empty terrace.
A stripped bicycle chained to a lamppost.

Having neither hut nor pond, let's stay
in this room and cultivate gentleness.

Machines will do the sorting and remembering.
Machines will run the kidneys and the lottery,
insert the repeat lines in their places:

No one can take your loneliness.

*

Read of the monumental eros
of the dead, read
the wildflower identification book all winter.

She held a dripping sponge
in the doorway, saying goodbye.

A bottle fell from a drunk's pack, didn't break.

"Imagine you are guarded by chance."

It was like a dream of rain falling
into an unfinished cathedral
to one from a country of extractable minerals.

*

To find what heroes missed,
I wander not far.

The river squeezes through
the broken locks. Wanderers toss dice
against the cracked abutments.
My secrets are not different
from the secrets of the others:

It's easier to pile rocks than watch a cloud very long.
Taught to solve for x, but not to taste food.
Taught by the older children

to throw sharp stones at slow-dying spawning
black salmon.

To find what heroes missed, I sit watching the river
compelled to leap its hurdles endlessly.

*

Stars over gravel
a cat sunned on earlier,
your your

is as first raindrops
on paving stones, as

cloud-break sunlight
through a train window shows
the fiery transparency
of a sleeping child's eyelids.

No one can take your loneliness.

*

I admire that emperor,
I forget which,

who, asked to return
from a far province to the throne demurred,
"I'd rather stay here and grow cabbages."

But having neither plot nor packet
of dragon's teeth, Pythagorean

past lives nor opinion
why seashells are found sometimes
on the slopes of peaks, I merely imitate

what I do not intend
to improve upon, whatever rough

or folded shows the impetus written into it
against entropy:

the cut cabbage cascading through itself,
the vertiginous rude crag
intended as mere background to the conversion scene,

whose knotty stylization kept me a long time in that gallery.

In the Shadow of the Reactor

God of Grids,
hear my attention.

Winged seeds spin down
into counter-
spinning
eddies,

likeness fled
awe-soon.

Show me a battery as yet
can store it,
awe.

From the dry riverbed of this
language's end,
what was
maple

rises utterly.

Litany

I am with you where no preference is
Sunlight climbs the nail
I am a with a with   not a you
where the ice has gone

Two planes fly over
a deer skeleton dug up
I am with you where no preference is   la la

A book of light crosses
the forest floor   I cannot
read in receptors all down my length   nevertheless

I am a with
the blue absolutely
through the pales of the corn rattles inaugurates

Flattened vole,
the stair metaphor has taken the schools,
a nut rebounds from a stone
as if a great caution about occurrences suddenly
was not

and I was a with   held
in the swept pile of the hair of many heads
the hair of the stem of the coneflower
of the beardtongue

speaking nevertheless
no preference be with you   as I am

by a stream that doesn't even keep
any course or calendar
listening to its un-listening

I learned it on this pilgrimage to the Middle
from two great ones who looked up from the ribs
of the owl they were eating, I learned to be a with, largely

the rooms in any glance   you can't go in

Marshy ravine your one week of unprepossessing raggy rustishness
like lit storefronts dark closes down around
the instruments searching out conditions miss

like a friend's face
in the face of an ancient
statue brought up from the bottom of a lake
the museum's closed-circuit cameras are closed to

like scent of winter's broken branches sawn in segments
warming in the sun welcome as

one who greeted us tenderly in childhood
with the unplanned obsolescence of all
rains

Rain turning to snow across the stadium lights be with you
"Rifle-Range Impact Area" on a fence of tangled purples be with
you data collectors banding kestrels ankles be with
you line-up of planes hanging over the dusk-colored lake be with
you emptiness that displaces very water

Havening

We are each
other's not safe.

Breath is you slip
from the image

of you. The pulse
at your neck

is shocking.
Touches my

touched eyes.
You

of the
roe-small,

freckler
of vacancy.

Be given,
not partial;

the world is
no-sided.

Unfastening

As a cicada pupa nails its clawed shell to a post
and, winged, escapes itself, we clawed
and left our bodies on the bed.

Fell back, feet in the comforter's cold
lake-bottom muck,
debris around our eyes at the waterline.

A walnut fruit thudded the roof
and instantly countless roots held the house up.

Roll over. What does it fasten
if we pull? The long
silts filter. The blinds go

the color of sleep in a raft,
and I complain beauty is
a book-word now like *undreggy*,

but you know better, or feel better, rather,
remembering the one

who laid his small all, his full
human length down on a dry road before rain

to leave a figure he
could stand to see
disappearing.

Coat

Far snag, small turtle
brushing flies from its face

You unshelled—
your hair floats strangely
in your child-bath bodily trance

Put on your coat, let's go
again among snakes and turtles, oaks, the us
there's no pronoun for

Your coat, someday, a doll's coat
in a box I open   I close again   give away
this day   that day

Ah, son, what my own father could not explain
for all he tried—

your coat

Aftercast

She would recall aspen-silver winds
on the river ridge   giving birth to him

My son my suddenly

Imagine a
mosquito having a name

"I've been hiding the hurt part,
the part that's most alive…"

Under the bridge a woman peels
a massive root on the overturned bottom of a box
A man sits next to her with his shirt off

My suddenly   my grown son

the strangeness of having known
anyone

a cloud flashes
through a pooled tire-tread

In the Preserve

Blinds of the half-demolished building blew openly.

I entered through the arch lit by sere leaves.

Lightning flashed in the icicles.

C played the Pathetique unfamiliar.

I lay on the rectangle of our collective imagining.

Against the canceled vastness.

Come back to this season if you can get past Hope.

See lead from Roman forges in bubbles in Arctic ice.

An alien oak under a cat's cradle of cables.

Where ditch and river meet.

Some breakthroughs of sun flashing the panels.

Loneliness of wood smoke and a radio.

Rain when you fell asleep, snow when you woke.

C said it was like visiting another country.

Mounds of frozen waves brought the horizon close.

The creek trickled through the canted slabs.

As sunlight resists us somewhat.

I ripped the leatherette cover from a journal given to me.

Admired the dried glue swirled unselfconsciously by hand.

Deep melt in the ditch-pond doubled sunset.

A swallow gathered beyonds on a peeled branch.

Each thing presented itself out of all of its seasons.

Snow crumbled like yellow flecks of glue from an old binding.

Thick brush broke open a shack and let sky in.

The river sieved through a metal shopping cart.

That was the bottom of the dream.

C said we live no other.

A pocket of snowflakes changed direction like a school of herring.

Snow is falling missed more motions than I could make it mean.

The fool only gives the others back to themselves.

A scarecrow, chrome globe for a head.

Seven stories of casino parking by the filtration plant.

Thirty trailers of coarse salt.

Cell phone birdsong with its one meaning.

Everything you see is paid for.

The guru breathing into the microphone after it's over.

Thoreau attributed to Hawthorne.

A hat-less acorn.

Frost like dominoes on the same side of every stem.

A law there's no following.

I followed an oak-leaf's footprint across new snow.

Found a windy dune like a struck tuning fork haloing itself.

Went to gather alone to bring to C.

She was everywhere like cloudshadow bending the grasses.

Unverifiable and utterly.

Out of the vastness without trespass.

A glacial tone, a cloud-and-water surround.

A boarded-up school holding open echoes.

A blue flame under a tea kettle hovering on a branch in a window.

The prisoner of war picnic shelter empty at that hour.

Snow falling through streetlights and headlights.

What any evening I may come out and have all to myself.

A motion sensor tripped by lichen dilating in moonlight.

What any morning I may come out and have all to myself.

Different bird song on either side the house.

Simplicity Patterns on a factory freaked with vines.

Pieces of hail striking the cable, bouncing off in loopy trajectories.

Gulls resting on the pond-ice's melt-margin.

Huge old oaks following a lost road through thin new growth.

A snarl of grass and twigs where something lives under the eaves.

In the House of Long Views.

Listened to the Om of the refrigerator.

From a window watched screens flashing in other windows.

Sun rose from a chimney.

Ago crept like cloudshadow o'er.

A daughter led her daughter through the falling flakes across.

Gentleness as much.

I brought it when I could.

I brought whatever had fallen across my path.

The creek's lights guttering.

Liquor bottles and wrappers of a rabbit's habitat.

A man shoveling, his dog leaping to meet the leaping snow.

Motions not me that became me.

A man stood in a doorway watching until a woman drove away.

The bones dissolve on their own in the gold cans.

An agreement made on our behalf.

C said we could get away with watching the heron that close to the plant.

I said it was like visiting another country.

Attention being of a kind.

Being without kind or degree.

No way to say it utterly.

The rain has dash the rain has down.

A snail is safe from hail.

Purple yellow.

Sugar maples stand as if they revolved around the sun.

C welcomes me at January's door.

In the silence of cars passing and a far helicopter.

A swallow drinking melt out in the namelessness.

ACKNOWLEDGMENTS

The author is grateful to the journals where poems in this collection first appeared:

32 Poems, AGNI, Antioch Review, BOMB, The Bombay Gin, Carolina Quarterly, Chicago Review Online, Cincinnati Review, Cold Mountain Review, Colorado Review, Commonweal, Conjunctions, Cortland Review, Crazyhorse, Cream City Review, Denver Quarterly, DIAGRAM, Dusie, Faultline, FIELD, Hampden-Sydney Poetry Review, Harpur Palate, Interim, The Journal, Louisville Review, Matter, The Minnesota Review, Minnetonka Review, North American Review, North Dakota Quarterly, Notre Dame Review, RHINO, Seneca Review, Shenandoah, South Dakota Review, Sou'wester, The Spoon River Poetry Review, Third Coast, Verse Daily, Washington Square Review, and *Witness.*

The author is also grateful to the presses that first published the books in this collection:

Magnifier, The Center for Literary Publishing, 2019
In the Gorge, Codhill Press, 2017
Invasives, New Rivers Press, 2014
Source to Mouth (chapbook), New Michigan Press, 2012

Finally, the author would like to express deep gratitude to:

Dr. Ross Tangedal, Brett Hill, and all of the Cornerstone Press editors for their painstaking care and attention to bring out this book;

Stephanie G'Schwind at the Center for Literary Publishing, Pauline Uchmanowicz at Codhill Press, Suzzanne Kelley at New Rivers Press, and Ander Monson at New Michigan Press for first publishing books selected from in this collection and for their encouragement.

Evan Summer for providing the sublime cover image for this book.

Bill Olsen and Nancy Eimers for insight and support that helped shape this book; Richard Kenney, Heather McHugh, and Roger Gilbert for the lasting influence of their teaching.

Friends whose talk and work has been sustaining: Glenn Shaheen, Laurie Cedilnik, Elizabyth Hiscox, Douglas Jones, Andrew Weissenborn, Scott Bade, Franklin K.R. Cline, Olivia Clare, T. Zachary Cotler, Michael Rutherglen, David Welch, Pattabi Seshadri, Alex Walton, Avery Slater, Steve Dold, Lacey Henson, Sean Clemmons, Kevin Craft, Katie Ogle, Sierra Nelson, Rebecca Hoogs, Johnny Horton, Will Bernhard, Carol Light, Joshua Beckman, Matt Dube, Stephanie Carpenter, Emily Robbins, Jeff Allen, Jeff Voccola, Andy Vogel, Robb Fillman, Cherri Buijk, Caroline Manring, Margaret Noel, Kenny Wachtel, Kevin McCloskey,

Evan Summer, and the whole crew of poets at the Vargtimmen King Koffee open mic in Emmaus, Berks Bards in Reading, and Firefly Bookstore in Kutztown.

My family, for their love and support, especially Colleen and Ezra for cultivating a shared writing practice and life with me.

BRANDON KRIEG is the author of *Magnifier*, winner of the 2019 Colorado Prize for Poetry. His other poetry collections are *In the Gorge* (2017), *Invasives* (2014), and a chapbook, *Source to Mouth* (2012). Two of his collections were finalists for the ASLE Book Award in Environmental Creative Writing and his work will be featured in *Attached to the Living World: A New Ecopoetry Anthology*, forthcoming from Trinity University Press. He grew up in Tualatin, OR, and now lives with his family in Kutztown, PA, where he teaches at Kutztown University.